# The Time Detectives

Terry Deary trained as an actor before turning to writing full time. He has many successful fiction and non-fiction children's books to his name, and is rarely out of the bestseller charts.

Other titles in the series:

# The Time Detectives

Book 1

# THE WITCH OF NIGHTMARE AVENUE

## TERRY DEARY

Illustrated by Martin Remphry

*faber and faber*

To Colin Anderson. A true supporter.

First published in 2000
by Faber and Faber Limited
3 Queen Square London WCIN 3AU

Origination: Miles Kelly Publishing
Printed in Italy

A CIP record for this book
is available from the British Library

ISBN 0-571-20107-5

# Contents

# The Time Detectives
# All about us

These are the files of the toughest team ever to tackle time-crime. We solve mysteries of the past, at last – and fast.

We are the Time Detectives.

My name is Bucket.

Katie Bucket. Commander of the Time Detectives.

And here is my squad. I wrote the secret files myself so you know they're true. Trust me...

Number: TD 001
Name:

Katie Bucket

Appearance:

Gorgeous, beautiful and smart.
The slightly scruffy clothes and messy
hair are just a disguise to fool the
enemy.

Report:

Katie Bucket is the boss,
Grown-ups always make her cross.
She's the Time Detectives' leader.
Cos she's brainy they all need her!

Special skills:

Cunning, brave, quick-thinking. Really
I'm too modest to tell you just how
great I am.

Hobbies:

Playing football, wrestling snakes,
making trouble. (It's a full-time hobby
just being so popular!)

Favourite victim:

Miss Toon our teacher.

Catch-phrase:

"Trust me, I know what I'm doing."

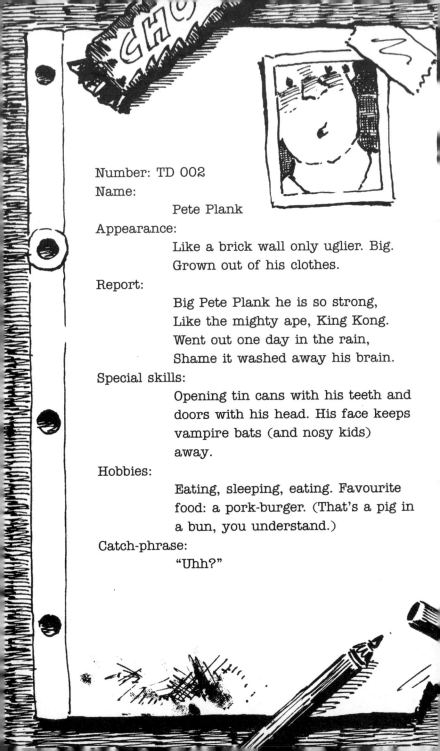

Number: TD 002
Name:
Pete Plank

Appearance:
Like a brick wall only uglier. Big.
Grown out of his clothes.

Report:
Big Pete Plank he is so strong,
Like the mighty ape, King Kong.
Went out one day in the rain,
Shame it washed away his brain.

Special skills:
Opening tin cans with his teeth and
doors with his head. His face keeps
vampire bats (and nosy kids)
away.

Hobbies:
Eating, sleeping, eating. Favourite
food: a pork-burger. (That's a pig in
a bun, you understand.)

Catch-phrase:
"Uhh?"

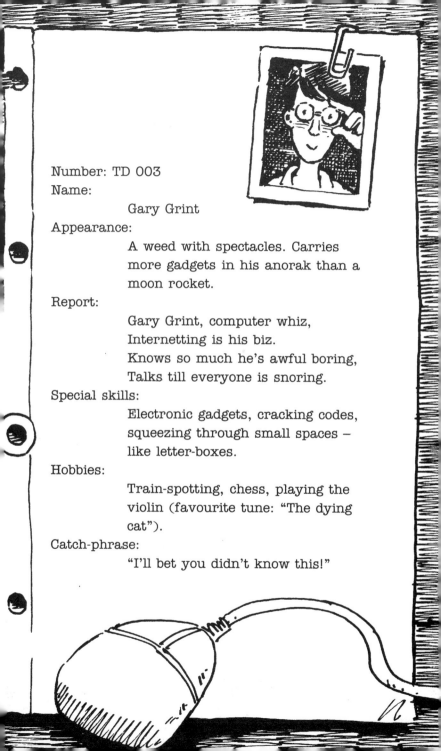

Number: TD 003
Name:

Gary Grint

Appearance:

A weed with spectacles. Carries
more gadgets in his anorak than a
moon rocket.

Report:

Gary Grint, computer whiz,
Internetting is his biz.
Knows so much he's awful boring,
Talks till everyone is snoring.

Special skills:

Electronic gadgets, cracking codes,
squeezing through small spaces —
like letter-boxes.

Hobbies:

Train-spotting, chess, playing the
violin (favourite tune: "The dying
cat").

Catch-phrase:

"I'll bet you didn't know this!"

Number: TD 004
Name:

Mabel Tweed

Appearance:

So squeaky clean you could eat your
dinner off her shining shoes. She's all
posh frocks and white socks.

Report:

Mabel Tweed is so good,
So polite and sweet as pud.
Does her homework neat and quick,
Teacher's pet. She makes me sick!

Special skills:

Creeping, grovelling and being
smarmy. I only let the lucky kid join
TDs cos her dad's a millionaire.

Hobbies:

Tidying her room, polishing her bike,
running errands for adults. Favourite
place: at Miss Toon's feet.

Catch-phrase:

"Do excuse me."

# Chapter 1
# The man who bashed his head on a crane

Pete Plank put his big paw in the air. "Please, Miss," he said. "What are we doing for Hallowe'en?"

Miss Toon looked over the top of her glasses and said, "Ignoring it, I hope."

Some of the class groaned. "We was looking forward to seeing you turn Pete into a toad, Miss Toon!" Gary Grint grinned.

But I wanted to know why she'd said that. "What's wrong with Hallowe'en, Miss?"

The teacher turned to me and raised her eyebrows. "It's all superstitious nonsense, Katie. The witches you read about in fairy tales don't exist. They never did!"

"What?" Pete gasped. He looked disappointed. "It said in today's newspaper there's a witch living here in our town – down Nightmare Avenue!" He pulled the newspaper from his school bag and waved the page at her. The class crowded round to look at it...

# The Duckpool Daily News

30th October

55p

# Witch's Curse Conks Crane Man

BY OUR STAFF REPORTER

CRANE operator, Doug Down, (33) was today nursing a sore head after a freak accident cracked his cranium and almost killed him. Mr Down had just knocked down the last house but one in Lord Mayor Avenue when elderly Mrs Googie Goonwilde leaned out of her window and screamed a curse at him. Mrs Goonwilde lives in the last house in Lord Mayor Avenue and is refusing to move. "She leaned out of her

*Mr Down*

*Mrs Goonwilde*

window, waved her broomstick at me and shouted a curse," Mr Down said from his sick-bed today. "She said, 'Bad luck to you and all your wicked machines!' Then, next thing I knew the crane suddenly sprang into life and the big ball on the end smacked me in the ear. Only me hard hat saved me! My mates reckon she's a witch. We'll be watching number 13 on Hallowe'en," he added. "People reckon they've seen her flying her broomstick. In the old days they used to burn witches! Pity they've stopped!"

Duckpool mayor, Mr Walter Weed (52), told the Duckpool Daily News, "The woman's a sad case. We've offered her money to move, so we can build a new road. Lots of money. Lots and lots and lots of money. But she refuses. She says she'll stay there till she dies. We hope she sees sense soon."

Mrs Googie Goonwilde told Duckpool Daily News that she owns the house and no one can force her to move. Our reporter asked her how she plans to stop the demolition team and she replied, "Look what happened to the last feller that came too close!"

■ Now turn to page 24 to see the exciting Duckpool Daily News Witch Fact File!

*The last house standing in Lord Mayor Avenue*

Miss Toon sighed. "Last half-term we studied the Tudors, remember? Well, in those days every village had their own 'cunning man' or 'wise woman' or 'sorcerer' or 'witch'. They were useful to have around. They'd cast spells to help the villagers. Look, here's a list of what they did," she said and wrote them on her whiteboard...

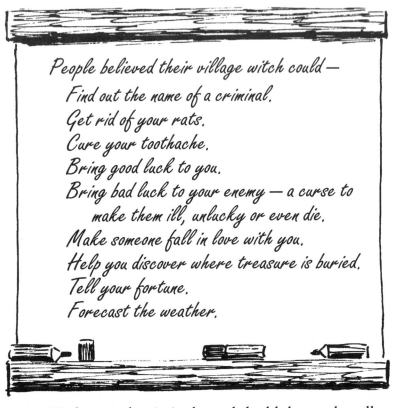

People believed their village witch could—
Find out the name of a criminal.
Get rid of your rats.
Cure your toothache.
Bring good luck to you.
Bring bad luck to your enemy — a curse to
    make them ill, unlucky or even die.
Make someone fall in love with you.
Help you discover where treasure is buried.
Tell your fortune.
Forecast the weather.

"Police catch criminals, and the bloke on the telly forecasts the weather," Gary Grint said. "Are they all witches?"

"And horoscopes in the newspaper tell your fortune," I agreed.

"Of course not," Miss Toon said. "But towards the end of the Tudor period people started to turn against witches and blame them for everything that went wrong. A dead cow, a bad harvest, a deadly disease – even burnt bread – were blamed on a witch's curse."

"Or a cracked head – like the man in the newspaper," Gary put in.

Miss Toon looked pleased. "Exactly, Gary. This Lord Mayor Avenue case looks like the Pendle Witches all over again. Look, here's a page from an old book on witchcraft..."

She placed the book face-down on her projector and showed it on the whiteboard behind her...

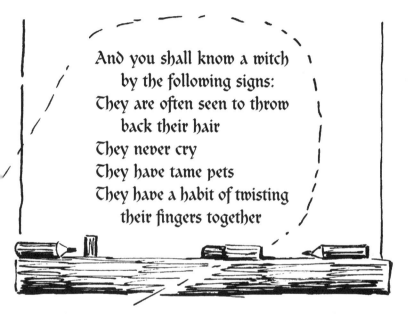

And you shall know a witch
by the following signs:
They are often seen to throw
back their hair
They never cry
They have tame pets
They have a habit of twisting
their fingers together

Miss Toon looked at us. "The pets were called 'familiars' and they were supposed to be witches' tame devils – how many of you have pets?" Most of the class put their hands up. "And you, Alice Winter, you throw back your hair – I've never seen you cry, Judy Johnson, even when you ran into the netball post last term. And George Thompson, you're forever twisting your fingers. I guess any one of us could be accused of being a witch! That's why I say it was a silly superstition. And, for some, it was deadly."

"But who were those Pendle Witches, Miss?" I asked.

Miss Toon is young and clever... and very mean. "Katie Bucket," she said. "I am the teacher and it is my job to ask the questions. If you want to know about the Pendle Witches then you will have to become a Time Detective and find out. You have computers and books and anything else you need. Before Hallowe'en I expect you to be able to answer my questions."

Clever teacher. The words "Time Detectives" had me hooked. I was going to be doing school work and enjoying it.

# Chapter 2
# The king who wiped his nose on his sleeve

"Won't you even give me a clue to get started?" I begged the teacher.

"Pendle is in Lancashire, in the north-west of England. And the trials took place in 1612, when King James was on the throne," she said and I scribbled the facts down. She opened a map-book and showed me...

"Do I have to do this by myself?" I asked.

"Who do you want to help?" Miss Toon asked.

"I'll have Gary Grint because he's a whiz with computers..."

I looked around the class where hands were going up and straining to touch the ceiling. "Me, Katie! Pick me!" The only one who didn't have his hand up was Pete Plank. Pete isn't very bright and no-one would ever pick him – not even to feed the class hamster.

"I'll pick Pete Plank," I said and my clueless classmates groaned. Pete looked surprised and puzzled and pleased all at the same time.

"You ought to have picked me," said a small girl in the world's shiniest shoes with the world's most polished face. Mabel Tweed. "I have the whole of Duckpool Town Council at my service. My daddy's the mayor, you know."

"I'd rather pick my nose than pick you," I said.

Mabel turned red and was about to reply angrily when Miss Toon cut in, "Talking about picking noses... that's just what I was going to talk about today!"

That twisting teacher had done it again. The quarrel was forgotten as we turned to hear more. "Last half-term we studied the Tudors – from Henry VII to Elizabeth I," Miss Toon reminded us. "This half-term we'll be looking at the family that followed. The Stuarts. Queen Elizabeth died with no children, so her nephew, who was king of Scotland, took the crown of England as well. His name was James."

Pete was staring out of the window, dreaming. Miss Toon said, "Who took Elizabeth's crown, Pete?"

Pete turned red. "Uhh?"

"Who took Elizabeth's crown?"

"Please, Miss, it wasn't me!"

Mabel Tweed sniggered unkindly. She said, "It was James."

Pete looked at James Jones sitting next to him and his mouth fell open. "James? What did you want to go pinching a crown for? You'll get into big trouble you will."

Miss Toon rubbed her eyes. "Never mind, Pete. Now, Mabel Tweed! Turn to page 11 and read what a French visitor called Fontenay said about James when he was 18 years old."

Mabel placed her shiny shoes on the floor and stood. She smiled at the class and cleared her throat with a little cough. She read...

"James Stuart had a straggling brown beard and hair, watery blue eyes and spindly legs. He was of middle height, more fat because of his clothes than his body. His clothes always being made large and easy, the doublets quilted to be dagger-proof. His breeches were in great pleats and full stuffed. He was naturally timid, his eyes large and always rolling after any stranger came into his presence. His beard was very thin. His tongue too large for his mouth which made him drink very badly as if eating his drink which came out into the cup from each side of his mouth. His skin was soft because he never washed his hands, only rubbed his finger ends slightly with the wet end of a napkin."

Mabel's voice became faint as she read the more disgusting parts. Miss Toon smiled to herself. "And those were just his good points!" the teacher said. "The French visitor forgot to mention James was bow-legged and picked his nose. The king used his sleeve instead of a handkerchief…"

Mabel sat down heavily.

"Just goes to show," I said. "Even posh people are human."

"Even kings," Gary Grint said.

"Even mayors, I suppose," I added, looking at Mabel. Her mouth was tight as a rat-trap.

"Up till break-time you can draw a picture of James from the description," Miss Toon said.

Here's mine. I've always been a brilliant artist...

When the bell went for break Miss Toon called out, "We can divide into groups after break and look at different parts of Stuart history. Katie's Time Detectives already know what they are doing..."

"Do we?" I asked.

"Yes," Miss Toon said. "You are going to look at witchcraft in King James's day – and especially the Pendle Witches."

It sounded like hard work. I didn't know it was also going to be dangerous...

That break-time we went into the playground – even though it was freezing. Have you noticed how teachers stay in the warm staffroom while we have to suffer like little Scotts of the Antarctic? Only our headteacher, Mr 'Potty' Potterton, was on duty and he had his hands wrapped around a pot of steaming tea.

Mabel Tweed spent most of break in a corner of the playground, talking on her mobile phone to someone; talking and looking towards me a bit too much.

Gary and I took Pete's newspaper and studied the special Hallowe'en page.

# Witch Fact File

HEY kids, Hallowe'en tomorrow night! Want to look like a REAL witch? Our ace fact-finders have dug into the books in the local library and come up with this description from Canada:

"Where have I seen that face before?" I asked, looking at the illustration beside the article.

"In a mirror," Gary Grint said stupidly.

"On the front page," Pete said – intelligently.

I turned back to the article on the old woman in Nightmare Avenue. It certainly looked a lot like her! "Well done, Pete," I said.

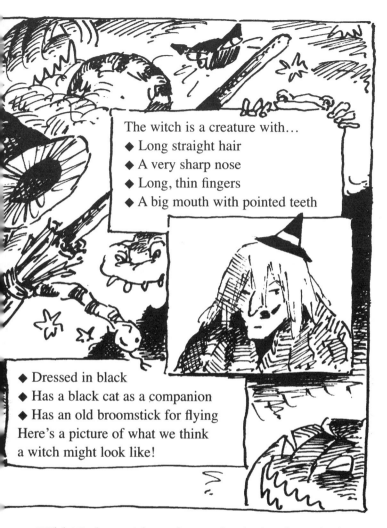

The witch is a creature with…
◆ Long straight hair
◆ A very sharp nose
◆ Long, thin fingers
◆ A big mouth with pointed teeth

◆ Dressed in black
◆ Has a black cat as a companion
◆ Has an old broomstick for flying
Here's a picture of what we think
a witch might look like!

"Uhh?" he said. I don't think he heard those words "well done" too often.

"Why would the newspaper do that? It's almost as if they want Mrs Goonwilde to be accused of being a witch," I said. I didn't know then how true that was.

# Chapter 3
# How to test a witch

"Maybe that Mrs Goonwilde is a witch," Pete said.

"Nah! Miss Toon said there's no such thing," I argued.

"Maybe she's miss-taken," Gary chipped in. Gary loved jokes. Pity he wasn't any good at telling them.

The bell rang for the end of break and Potty Potterton lined us up. Someone bumped me and I felt a hand slide into my pocket – a pickpocket! But, when I checked the pocket there wasn't anything missing. There was something extra there. Someone had slipped a note in.

In a quiet corner of the classroom I took it out. It was written on school notepaper and I showed it to Pete and Gary...

Dear Katie Bucket,
    I think you and your Time
Detectives may be able to help
me. My Granny Goonwilde is in
trouble. Can you come to number
13 Lord Mayor Avenue – the one
the kids call Nightmare Avenue –
tonight, October 30th, at 8:00.
You can't miss the house. It's the
only one the council haven't
knocked down.
    Yours in desperation.
        Ellie Goonwilde

P.S. Come in secret. They'll be
watching.

"That's the old lady accused of witchcraft!" Gary said. "Ellie's the girl that sits in the corner of our class and never says a word."

"She's hardly ever here!" I reminded him.

"How can we help?" Pete asked.

"We go and talk to her," I said. "But not in school. At her granny's home like she asked."

"Nightmare Avenue! At night!" Gary gasped. "Er... I've got the witchcraft research to do!"

"Fine," I said. "I'll take Pete with me. He's tougher than a school-dinner sausage!"

"Uhh?" he said. "Actually, Katie…"

"You can be my bodyguard, Pete," I told him. "But first we need to get ourselves armed!"

"Please can you arm me with a machine-gun?" Pete asked.

"No, Pete. I mean armed with facts." I turned to Gary Grint. "Can you find us some information about these Pendle Witches?"

"I know how a witch tells the time!" he said with his stupid grin.

I knew I shouldn't ask. But Pete did. "So how does a witch tell the time, Gary?"

"She has a witch-watch… wrist-watch, geddit?"

"Uhh? No, Gary," Pete frowned.

Gary looks and acts like a clown who has had his brain removed – until you sit him in front of a computer screen. Then his fingers fly over the keys and he can come up with the answer to almost any question – except for, "Where do flies go in the winter?"

We left him to get on with it while Pete and I looked in books that would help us. By lunch-time we had made a good start and showed Gary what we'd come up with.

Here's the way they used to test for witches, I said, pushing the book in front of him.

## Testing a witch by ducking

It is a well-known fact that a witch cannot drown. Water is used by Christians to baptise people. Water is pure. A witch cannot stand the touch of water. And water cannot stand the touch of a witch.

If a witch is thrown into water then the water will push upwards and he or she will float. If the suspect is innocent then he or she will sink.

To test your witch:

§ first tie his or her right thumb to the largest toe of the left foot
§ place the suspected witch in a sack and fasten the sack
§ throw the sack into a river or pond
§ if the witch floats they are guilty – take them out and execute them

If the witch sinks they are innocent – if they are still alive after the ducking then let them live.

"Is that how they tried the Pendle Witches?" I asked.

Gary pushed his round spectacles back on his nose and looked clever. "No, they just took them to Lancaster Castle, locked them in a freezing dungeon for a month or two and then took them to court. I discovered that there was only one report of their trial ever written. And I've printed a copy from the computer," he said.

I looked at the printout. The title of the book was…

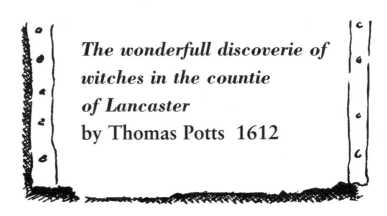

*The wonderfull discoverie of witches in the countie of Lancaster*
by Thomas Potts  1612

"What do you know about this Thomas Potts?" I asked Gary.

"I know he can't spell!" Gary laughed. I pulled a face but stopped my hands from shaking him warmly by the throat.

"Look, it's not just what's written in the books that's important. We have to know about the writers. I mean, that old King James wrote about witches because he thought they were attacking him. You can't trust what he says! How do we know we can trust Thomas Potts?"

Gary shrugged. "I'll do a computer search, but I can tell you one thing about him... he had some very strange ideas. Look what he says on the opening page..."

He passed the printout to me. The lines were marked:

The wrinkles on an old woman's face show most people that she is a witch.

Pete Plank blinked. "Uhh? That means most of our teachers are witches! Ooooh-errrr!"

"No, Pete," I told him. "It just means this Thomas Potts was as stupid as the reporter for the Duckpool Daily News."

"You mean it's not true?"

"I mean I don't believe it. There's only one way the Time Detectives are going to find the whole truth."

"What's that, Katie?"

"It's to find out for ourselves. Meet me at seven on the corner of Nightmare Avenue," I told Pete.

"Is it safe?"

"Safe as houses."

"Which houses?" he asked.

"The houses on Nightmare Avenue," I told him.

"But Katie, they've all been knocked down!" he whimpered.

Good point. "You don't get much safer than that!" I told him.

"Uhh?" he said.

# Chapter 4
# Dead cats, boots and storms

And that's how we came to be in Nightmare Avenue on the night before Hallowe'en.

The night was dark... well, most nights are. But this one was darker because the street lamps were all out.

We two fearless Time Detectives stumbled through the rubble that spilled onto the pavement, guided by the smell of broken bricks and cracked concrete.

"Where are we? Uhh?" Pete Plank whispered.

"In Nightmare Avenue," I whispered back.

"Katie?" Pete whispered.

"What?" I hissed.

"Why are we whispering?"

"Because... because... because I say so. Trust me – I know what I'm doing!" I snapped. "Now, let me just check the message." I said. I reached into my pocket and found... crumbs from old crisps, a lot of fluff and a sheet of paper. I passed it to Pete because I was holding the torch. "What number is it again?"

I heard the paper rustle in the darkness – though it could have been a rustling rat scuttering over the ruined houses. "I don't know," Pete said. "I can't read a word."

"Your reading isn't good, Pete, but you can read a simple note like that," I sighed.

"Not in the dark, Katie."

I clicked the torch on. Little red eyes stared out from the shadows of the rubble and little white teeth chattered hungrily. I turned the torch on the note and blinked. "This isn't the note from Ellie Goonwilde!" I said. "Someone's pinched the note and put their school notes in its place so I wouldn't miss it!"

"Uhh? What does it say?" Pete asked.

I scanned the note. "It's Group Seven's worksheet – on King James's early life…"

# HISTORY WORKSHEET

Class *7DT.*

The Stuarts. King James (1603—1625)
Question: What can you find out about
James before he became King of England
in 1603?

ANSWER: *James was the son of Mary Queen*
*of Scots. She was a pretty nasty old bat who*
*had James's Dad murdered then married the*
*murderer. (I'm glad she's not my mum.)*
*Anyway the Scots booted her out and made*
*James king. He was just 13 months old at the*
*time! How did they find a crown to fit him?*

*Mary ran away to England where Queen*
*Elizabeth locked her up for 18 years then had*
*her head lopped off. Did you know, it took the*
*axe-man three goes to get the old bat's head*
*off? Chop, chop, chop.*

26

James had trouble with a witch when he was a young man. The Earl of Bothwell was powerful – and potty – and called himself "The Wizard Earl". The Wiz tried to kill James with witchcraft. When that failed, he tried to kill James with a sword. He attacked the young king in Holyrood House (that's his palace in Edinburgh in case you're interested). James locked himself in a room and probably wet himself before help came and rescued him. (Well, I would have wet myself.)

James went across to Denmark to marry Princess Anne (no, not the one we have today). On the way back to Scotland they were almost drowned when their ship was smashed by a terrible storm. It seems that a woman called Agnes Sampson and a group of witches had been throwing dead cats and bits of dead human bodies into the sea to raise the storm. (I suppose they got the human bits from the Body Shop and the moggies from a cat-alogue – Ha! Ha! That's a joke, Miss Toon!)

Anyway, James survived the storm, he heard about the plot and sent for the witches. He questioned their leader, Agnes Sampson. To his amazement the woman repeated to James some of the things he had whispered to his wife on the night of his wedding – words that no-one but James and Anne could have heard. James was gobsmacked and started to really believe in witches then. I can't say I blame him!

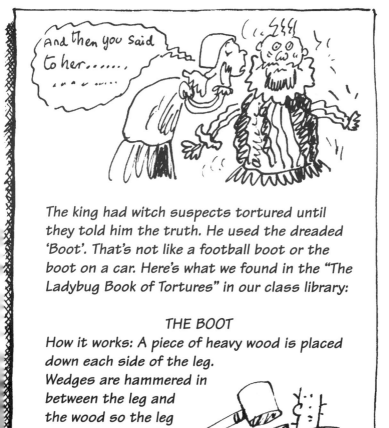

And then you said to her.......  .... .. .....

The king had witch suspects tortured until they told him the truth. He used the dreaded 'Boot'. That's not like a football boot or the boot on a car. Here's what we found in the "The Ladybug Book of Tortures" in our class library:

### THE BOOT

How it works: A piece of heavy wood is placed down each side of the leg. Wedges are hammered in between the leg and the wood so the leg is steadily crushed. In 1596 Thomas Papley was kept in a Boot for eleven days and nights, kept without any clothes in a freezing cell and whipped with birch twigs. Sounds worse than Miss Toon's detention, I reckon.

*King James was an especially nasty man –
just like our headmaster – but please don't
tell him I said that. Back in 1596 a man called
Bishop Burnet wrote. "When any man was
tortured in the Boot it happened in front of
the Council. Almost all of the councillors
wanted to run away. But James was far from
running away; in fact he watched carefully as if
he was watching an experiment. Everyone who
saw this got the impression that he was a
man without a drop of mercy."*

*James was so interested in witchcraft that
he wrote a book about it in 1597 called
"Demonology".*

"Ooooh! That's creepy!" Pete trembled. "Miss
Toon said there was no such thing as witches!"

"No, think about it, Pete," I told him. "If that
Agnes Sampson and her friends were really plotting
with the devil, how come the storm failed to sink

James's ship? Is the devil so feeble that he can't wreck a frail wooden vessel?"

"Uhh?" Pete said.

"Never mind. Remember what Miss Toon told us. Nasty neighbours can attack you just because they think you're a witch. That's why we're here! Now stop biting your nails."

"Got none left to bite, Katie. I've started biting yours!"

"Ouch!" I cried and snatched my hand away. I studied the papers again. "Whichever group did this they've done us a favour."

"Uhh?"

"We have to investigate a witch trial in James's England. These notes tell us James was interested in witchcraft up in Scotland. I'll bet he was just as interested in witchcraft when he came to England. Remember, Pete, a leopard never changes its spots."

"Uhh? Why?"

"Why what?"

"Why doesn't a leopard change its socks? My mum says I should change my socks every day or my feet will smell, my mum says and…"

"Pete!"

"Yes, Katie?"

"Shut up."

"Yes, Katie."

I flicked the torch beam over the piles of tumbled walls. One house stood alone in the darkness. It was tall and twisted with towers like a vampire's teeth.

There was a ghostly wail. "Oooo-ooooh!"

I shivered. Then I realised it was pathetically petrified Pete Plank. "Cut out the hanky-panky Planky and let's get this case cracked."

I opened the iron gate that led up the crazy-paving path that wound through bristling bushes. The front door was once green but now it was faded and peeling. The brass knocker was made in the shape of some hideous face from hell! "Hey!" Pete Plank gasped. "What's your face doing on that door knocker, Katie?"

I let it fall with a sharp rattle. Moments later there was a clatter of bolts and chains being loosened behind the door. Ellie Goonwilde had been waiting.

## Chapter 5
# Into the terror of Nightmare Avenue

The girl was tall and fat – heavier than even Pete Plank. Her pasty face looked at us, lit by a flickering candle. "Thanks for coming," she sighed.

She swung the door open a little further and stood aside to let us in. Suddenly a voice called from the gate at the end of the path. "I say! Do excuse me!"

We swung round. "Uh?" Pete grunted.

Even in the dim light of the candle her bicycle glinted a rich gold. Her hub-caps were chrome and her frilled dress was shimmering white. Golden ringlets framed her scrubbed-bright face.

She propped the bike on its golden stand and marched up the path towards us, a white leather bag swinging from her shoulder. It was Mabel Tweed, the richest and snobbiest girl in Miss Toon's class. "I say... you lower-class people! What are you up to?"

"Visiting a friend, beady Tweedy. What's it to you?" I asked.

She ignored me and looked over my shoulder at Ellie Goonwilde. "I say, you rather overweight girl. Isn't this the witch's house?"

"No!" Ellie sobbed suddenly. "It's not true! She's not a witch!"

Mabel Tweed reached into her shoulder-bag and took out a newspaper. "That's what it says in this morning's Duckpool Daily News, so it must be true, large girl!"

I snatched the paper from her and read it while Mabel Tweed looked over my shoulder.

I looked at Mabel Tweed hard. "That's your dad, Mayor Walter Tweed, isn't it?"

"He's a millionaire, you know," she smirked.

"He's a bully. Trying to drive an old lady out of her home," I told her.

"Do excuse me," Mabel said, fluttering her long curling eyelashes. "But Daddy is offering her money – lots and lots and lots of money – not threatening her. Bullies don't offer their victims money!"

I couldn't think of an answer to that so I gave it. "———"

Ellie Goonwilde gave a great groan. "But he doesn't have to threaten her. The newspaper's done it for him."

"The newspaper doesn't say anything nasty," Pete Plank said.

"Look at page 24!" Ellie begged. I found the right page…

"Don't worry, Ellie," I said. "Only an utter idiot would think your gran looks like the picture of the witch."

"I think she does," Pete said.

I nodded. "Exactly."

Ellie Goonwilde led the way through the dark corridors of the old house. It smelled of unwashed spiders and the corpses of their victims. Dust rose in little clouds as we tramped up the stairs. Ellie turned, her pale face blushing. "It's hard for me to keep the house clean for Gran when there's no electricity," she said. "All I have is Gran's broomstick."

"And you won't have much time when you have to go to school," Pete Plank put in.

Ellie shook her large head. "I never go to school these days. Gran needs someone to look after her." She stopped on the landing and looked down at the floor. "Don't mind if Gran talks a little funny," she mumbled. "She's... she's getting old."

"I know just what you mean!" Mabel Tweed cried and clasped her white little hands around the newspaper as if she were praying. "Daddy often says strange things. He's a millionaire, you know."

I grabbed Mabel by the frill on the front of her frock. "Look, greedy Tweedy, we don't care if you and your daddy live in Buckingham Palace. We are here to help old Mrs Goonwilde. This is a Time Detectives' case."

"I know, tatty-haired girl," she said brightly. "And I've decided to join the Time Detectives! I can be a great help." She smiled at Ellie. "Now, large girl, lead on to the troubled wrinkly!" Mabel turned her round eyes on me. "And please release my ruffle before you dirty it with your rather grubby hands!"

"You will get my rather grubby fist in your nose if you're not careful!" I hissed.

"I don't think so. My daddy's the mayor, you know!"

"And I'm the leader of the Time Detectives... we solve mysteries of the past, at last – and fast. So do as you're told," I said and followed Ellie Goonwilde through the dark oak door.

The room was lit by a glowing fire that cast shadows across the dusty floor. A black cat sat in the hearth and blinked its traffic-light eyes at us and a broomstick was propped up in the corner. Old Googie Goonwilde stood over a cauldron that bubbled and hissed over the fire and stirred it. The words she muttered would send a chill through a polar bear. They were like something out of a spell book…

Even in the red glow of the fire Pete and Mabel looked pale and shocked. But Ellie Goonwilde just grinned. "Gran used to be a librarian," she said as if that explained anything.

Pete breathed, "Is that a real witch's spell?"

Spell for making Double Trouble

Fillet of a fenny snake,
In the cauldron boil and bake;
Eye of newt, and toe of frog,
Wool of bat and tongue of dog,
Adder's fork, and blind-worm's sting,
Lizard's leg and owlet's wing;
For a charm of powerful trouble
Like a hell-broth boil and bubble.
Double, double toil and trouble;
Fire burn and cauldron bubble.
Cool it with a baboon's blood,
Then the charm is firm and good.

The old woman turned from the pot and pointed a crooked finger at him – crookedly. "Shocking, boy. I'm shocked! What's this world coming to? In my day we all knew that spell, word for word, at our school. Don't they teach you that sort of thing today?"

"We don't go to a witch's school, elderly woman," Mabel sniffed.

"Neither did I, frilly-knickered girl! I went to Grott Street Elementary School and they taught us the poem there!" She sighed and stirred her brew with a wooden spoon then scooped some up and slurped it. She added some salt.

"They taught you witchcraft at Grott Street Primary?" I asked.

"No! No! No! They taught us all about great English writers!" Granny Goonwilde said. "That poem was written by William Shakespeare in his play *Macbeth*!"

"I knew that," Mabel lied.

"Anyone for soup?" the old woman asked suddenly. "Made with the vegetables from our own garden," Ellie said eagerly.

We sat around the table and sipped at the warming soup. "This eye of newt and toe of frog's very tasty," Pete Plank said, licking his bowl clean. I didn't bother telling him he had more chance of finding eye of potato and toe of turnip.

"So did this Shakespeare believe in witches?" I asked. "He didn't write fairy tales did he?"

"No," Mrs Goonwilde said happily. "But the king was a funny sort of feller. King James was daft about witches. Shakespeare wrote the *Macbeth* play to please him!"

"Do excuse my saying, but surely the king didn't believe in witches!" Mabel sneered.

"Believe in them?" Mrs Goonwilde cackled. "King James wrote a book all about them. He captured witches, he tortured them and he executed them. Around 1600, it was! I was a librarian. Look! James passed a law against witches. Here's the old law book!" the old woman said. She turned and burrowed in a dark corner of the room. She came up with an ancient, musty, leather-bound book. She placed it on the table and we looked at it by candle-light.

# IT IS hereby Decreed
## that *No person* may :

1. Make an agreement with an evil spirit.
2. Harm a living hvman or injvre Cattle.
3. Use a dead body for a Magic spell.
4. Mix a love potion.

---

THE pvnishment for **Witchcraft** shall be DEATH.

*On the order of*
His Majesty King JAMES

1604

"Dozens of poor people died because of those laws," Ellie said quietly.

I shook my head. "Don't worry. No-one's going to execute your gran for witchcraft today! No-one really believes in witches now!"

"I do!" Mrs Goonwilde said.

"Uhh?" Pete Plank gasped.

Ellie turned her round face towards us. "That's one of the problems! Not only do some people round here believe Gran's a witch... she sometimes believes it herself!"

"Do excuse me," Mabel butted in. "But how do you expect the Time Detectives to help?"

"I want you to prove that there's no such thing as witches – and that there never was! Prove it to Gran... and prove it to her enemies!"

"Easy!" Mabel Tweed said.

"Easy-peasy," Pete Plank said.

I just knew that if Pete said "easy", it was going to be to be very, very difficult.

## Chapter 6
# Mad dogs and sick cows

"You've only got twenty-four hours," Ellie Goonwilde said to us. She'd taken us to her bedroom, out of the way of her gran to talk. "Tomorrow night's Hallowe'en and I think people really will come to watch Gran fly on her broomstick. Have you got a plan?"

My brain was as empty as Pete Plank's soup bowl after he'd licked it clean. But a great leader never lets her troops know she's beaten. So I lied. "Trust me, I know what I'm doing. I have a plan," I said.

Ellie, Pete and Mabel turned their candle-lit faces towards me.

"Well?" Mabel asked.

"Very well, thank you. How are you?" I replied. She blinked. "What is it?"

"What's what?"

"What's your plan?"

"I'm glad you asked me."

"So tell me."

I cleared my throat and started to speak. "My plan... is to hold a great witchcraft trial!"

"Uhh?" Pete Plank grunted.

But Mabel clapped her small white hands. "Brilliant! We'll try out all the witchcraft spells. When people see how useless they are then they'll see what nonsense it all is!"

"Will they?" I asked.

"Do excuse me, Katie, dear. I never suspected you had such a great brain... for such an ill-dressed person," Mabel smiled. "You're even cleverer than Daddy... and he's the mayor, you know."

"Where do we start?" Pete asked.

Now Mabel had showed me the way I knew what to do next. "Ellie... your gran has books. Get them and find us some spells. Oh, and write a list of all the things witches are supposed to do."

Ellie hurried off to find some books and a pen. I turned back to my team. "I'll get our computer genius Gary Grint to look up the history of witches on the computer."

"What can I do?" Pete asked.

"Go to the local museum tomorrow morning and see what they've got there," I told him.

"And me?" Mabel asked eagerly. "I'm very rich, you know."

"You, Mabel, can be our witch! Get a costume..."

"Mummy's dressmaker will make me one," she nodded.

"Get a wig and the make-up…"

"Anything else?" she asked.

"One other thing," I said quietly and leaned towards her.

"What's that?"

I grabbed her frilled frock. "If I ever hear you call poor Ellie 'large' or 'overweight' again then you'll be the richest corpse in Duckpool. Got it?"

"But she is!" Mabel wailed. "And she's ugly! I've seen thinner, prettier sacks of potatoes!"

"And you are a stuck-up, spoiled little madam… but I would never be so cruel as to tell you. So keep your nasty opinions to yourself, Miss Tweed."

Mabel pouted and glared at me but she finally mumbled, "I will try."

Ellie came back and laid her list in front of us. I glanced at it and nodded. Some of the things that witches were supposed to do surprised even me. People are still trying to do them today!

"Brilliant, Ellie," I said. I took the list of spells from her and glanced at them.

# WITCH SPELLS

to cure madness... release a live
bat in the room of the sufferer

to find the name of a criminal...
write the names of suspects on
pieces of paper and wrap them
in balls of clay. Drop the clay
balls into a bucket. The one
that unwraps first will be the
guilty person

to cure a mad dog... feed it paper
with a charm written on it

to cure a headache... boil some of
the sufferer's hair in their
urine then throw it on a fire

to cure animal sickness... tie herbs
to the animal's tail or tap them
with a magic wand

to make someone fall in love with
you - scatter rose petals
across the path where they
are walking. They will fall in
love with the next person they
see

to cure aching bones - jump in a
river!

"Tomorrow we are going to have a witch trial," I said.

"Where?" Pete asked.

"In the front garden of this house! Miss Toon will like that. 'History in Action' she likes to call it! She will probably let the rest of the class watch!"

Little did I know that my witch trial would be watched by more than class 7DT. Because, after we'd said goodnight to Ellie Goonwilde, we stepped out of the door and into the dark garden. As we fumbled our way towards the gate there was a sudden explosion of brilliant light. It dazzled me and all I could see were purple and green spots in front of my eyes. For a minute I was sure I'd gone blind.

"What was that?" Pete cried.

"Just the flash from a camera," Mabel said happily. "I'm used to it – me being the daughter of the mayor, of course. My picture's in the paper all the time, you know."

But the picture that appeared in the Duckpool Daily News the next day was like nothing Mabel had ever seen before...

# Chapter 7
# Curses and trials

I stayed in the classroom at break-time the next morning. As Mabel tried to leave I stood in front of her and waved the newspaper under her snooty little nose. "What is this?" I asked her.

"Do excuse me, but I think it's obvious. It's a newspaper!" she said with a smirk.

"And why does this newspaper give away all our secrets?" I asked her. "Which traitor betrayed us?"

"I'm sure I don't know what you mean!" she replied. "I was only doing my public duty and talking to the press."

Our plan for a 'History in Action' event looked like turning into a 'Circus in Action' event...

# The Duckpool Daily News

31 October                    Still only 55p

## Time Detectives to Try Witch Tonight!

THE WITCH of Nightmare Avenue faces a horrible Hallowe'en showdown tonight, when pupils from Duckpool Primary hold a 'History in Action' event.

*Mabel Tweed and her top tec team leave the witch's house last night.*

Leading Time Detective, Mabel Tweed (daughter of the millionaire mayor Walter Tweed), spoke to our reporter last night from her mansion. "We plan to get to the bottom of this mystery once and for all. This will be the greatest witch trial since 1612!"

Dabbing tears from her well-scrubbed cheeks Mabel said, "This poor persecuted woman will be set free by my terrific team! We will prove that she is innocent!"

"Or guilty," her father added.

Our reporter spoke to witch-victim Doug Down, who told him, "I'll be there tonight with some of the

*Mr Down made inflammatory remarks.*

other lads. If she's found guilty then we'll know what to do." Our reporter asked the man with the smashed skull what he meant. "Mr Down replied, "In the old days they burned witches – me and the lads will have a box of matches with us. Know what I mean?"

Mayor Walter Tweed said, "It would be much easier if the old witch just let us move her to a new house. My council wants to see the new road built – but we don't really want to build it over Mrs Goonwilde's burned body, do we?"

The Duckpool Daily News will have a reporter there tonight!

Mabel shrugged. "Do excuse me but what we are doing tonight is not a secret. The more people who know about Mrs Goonwilde the better. If the whole town sees she is innocent, so much the better."

"And that's why you contacted the newspaper?" I asked.

The two-faced Mabel blushed – on both of her faces. She was guilty of betraying the Time Detectives' plan. The only thing that saved her miserable life was Gary Grint who came up to us with a bundle of papers. "Here you are, Katie! The reports on the Pendle Witches that you wanted."

I took them from him and spread them over the nearest desk. Gary explained, excitedly – so excitedly that his glasses began to steam up – "One of the women at the centre of the witchcraft was a widow called Alizon Device. And the poor woman just fitted the way people expected a witch to look!"

"As ugly as Mabel here?" I asked while the well-scrubbed girl glared at me.

"Even worse! Alizon Device had an uneven face with one eye higher than the other – one looked up and the other down. Imagine someone like that in our school."

I nodded. "They'd be picked on and bullied, I guess."

"Alizon and her children were so poor they had to go begging," Gary went on.

"That's not a crime," Mabel put in.

"No, but what happened on March 18th was!" Gary said eagerly. He pointed to a page that he'd printed out...

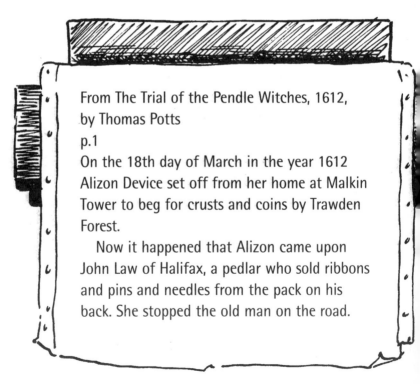

From The Trial of the Pendle Witches, 1612,
by Thomas Potts
p.1
On the 18th day of March in the year 1612
Alizon Device set off from her home at Malkin
Tower to beg for crusts and coins by Trawden
Forest.

Now it happened that Alizon came upon
John Law of Halifax, a pedlar who sold ribbons
and pins and needles from the pack on his
back. She stopped the old man on the road.

"Good day, Master Law," Alizon said.

The man stepped back a little afraid for he knew what the local folk said about Alizon and her family. He made the sign of the cross to protect himself and moved to walk past the young woman. "Good day, young Alizon."

She reached out a hand to stop him. "Sell me a packet of pins," she said.

"What would you want with pins?" the old man asked.

"I will sell them and make a little money," the young woman said.

"Let me see your money first," the pedlar said.

"I'll pay you when I've sold the pins," she promised.

The old man laughed and said, "I'd be a fool to believe the lies of a witch," and he walked past her.

When he was no more than ten paces past her he heard her cry, "The devil take you, John Law, you mean old sinner!"

Mabel sniffed. "That's not a crime! I could curse you, Katie Bucket, but that doesn't make me a witch! I could say, 'I hope you fall down stairs and break your neck!' – but there's nothing wrong with that!"

"Ah!" Gary cried. "But what if Katie fell down stairs and broke her neck?"

"She wouldn't," Mabel said crossly.

"But what if she did?" Gary insisted.

"Then it would just be bad luck," Mabel sighed.

"Mrs Goonwilde cursed the crane-driver and he had an accident," I reminded her.

"So what happened to the old pedlar?" Mabel asked.

Gary pushed the next sheet in front of her...

From The Trial of the Pendle Witches, 1612,
by Thomas Potts
p.2

The accused witch, Alizon Device, cursed the said John Law and went on her way. But shortly after the pedlar fell to the ground and was carried to a nearby alehouse.

The whole of his left side was lame and useless. He complained, "I feel as if I am being pricked by knives. This was done to me by witchcraft by Alizon Device!"

Later that day Alizon Device went to the alehouse, looked at her victim and then went away.

Mabel frowned. "Maybe the old man was just pretending to be sick. Maybe he was trying to get Alizon into trouble."

Gary shook his head. "Sorry, Mabel, but he went along to the trial to give evidence. He was crippled for life."

Mabel looked so cross I thought she was going to stamp her shiny little shoe and cry. Instead she thumped Gary's papers with her fist. "It isn't fair," she said. "All she had to do was say she never meant it. Say she wasn't a witch! That would have saved her from being burned! What happened to her?"

Gary peered at her through his glasses. "I don't know, Mabel. I haven't got to the end of the trial."

She turned on her heel and went towards the door.

"Where are you going?" I asked her.

"To prove Mrs Goonwilde not guilty!" she said.

"How?"

"That's my business," she said and lifted her button nose in the air.

"But I'm the leader of the Time Detectives!" I cried.

"But I am the daughter of the mayor!"

"So what?" I asked, but she had gone.

# Chapter 8
# The bad, burning bishop

Pete Plank wandered into the room and asked, "Where's Mabel off to in such a hurry?"

"How am I supposed to know?" I snapped.

Pete looked disappointed. "I thought you knew everything, Katie. After all, you're a detective."

"Yes!" Gary said. "You should be searching for clues and finding out what Mabel's up to."

"Yes – well – I was just going to!"

"You were probably going to start by searching her desk!" Pete said.

"Ah – oh – was I? Yes! Yes, Pete! How did you guess! That's just what I was about to do!"

I raised the lid of Mabel's desk. I have never in my life seen such a tidy desk! Not a blob of chewing-gum or a shaving from a pencil-sharpener in sight. Just a neat pile of books, each one neatly labelled. I picked up the one marked 'Witch Project' and opened it.

Mabel had been doing a lot of collecting. But one piece of writing caught my eye...

In Germany the Bishop of Wutzburg burned more than 900 witches at the stake in 8 years – including lawyers, priests, lords and children as young as seven – he even had his own nephew beheaded. But he grew very rich from taking the property of the executed victims.

Underneath was a note...

Phone Duckpool hospital - 345678

I tapped the exercise book with my finger. "I know where Mabel's gone," I said.

Pete grinned like a chimp in a banana factory. "You're brilliant you are, Katie."

"I know. I can't help it," I told him.

"So are we going to put Mrs Goonwilde on trial tonight the way we planned?" Gary asked.

"Yes. Everything's ready. Mabel can't do any harm, I guess. Gary – find out what happened to the Pendle Witches and print it out so I don't have to do it for homework. Bring it along tonight. Pete – meet me on the corner of Nightmare Avenue at sunset."

Sunset on Nightmare Avenue was brighter than daylight that Hallowe'en. Television crews had set up their powerful lights and flooded the ruined street with brilliant light. The mobile swimming-tank had been delivered and was filled with water that trembled in the chilly breeze.

Crowds of curious people were beginning to gather outside the railings – kids in witch masks and monster costumes carrying turnip lanterns played hide-and-seek over the rubble of the ruined houses. We pushed past.

I hurried to the back door and Ellie was waiting for me. "Oh, Katie! I'm glad you've come!" she moaned. "It's Gran..."

"She's innocent and I can prove it," I said and marched past her.

"But..." Ellie tried to tell me something.

"Her troubles are over," I said.

As Pete and I stepped into the candlelit gloom of the kitchen Gary Grint ran up and gasped, "Katie! I've done it! I've found out what happened to Alizon Device and the Pendle Witches."

"Yes, but Katie, I have to tell you something…"

"Later, Gary," I said as I followed Ellie into old Mrs Goonwilde's room.

Mrs Goonwilde was dressed in black and was mixing some leaves in a bowl. "Mrs Goonwilde," I said cheerfully. "If you'll come downstairs we can show the people outside that you're not a witch after all!"

The woman looked at me, puzzled. "Not a witch? Not a witch?"

"Not a witch," Pete parroted.

"Oh, me dears, but I cursed that crane feller and he smashed his head!" she chuckled.

"Just luck!" I told her.

"No, no! He smashed his head because I cursed him! I think I really do have witch powers!" she smiled.

"Uhh?" Pete gasped.

"That's what I was trying to tell you!" Ellie sighed.

"And that's what I was trying to tell you," Gary added, waving a new printout in front of my nose. "I'll bet you didn't know this!"

I held it up to the candle and read it…

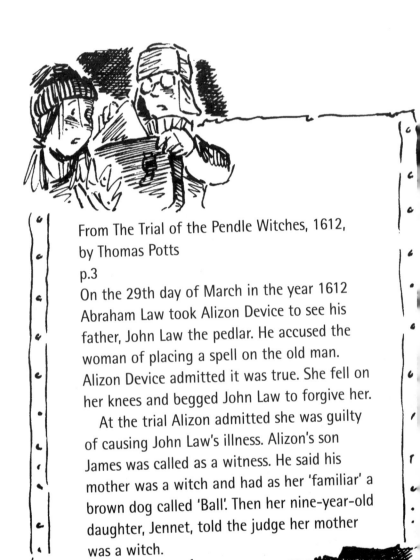

From The Trial of the Pendle Witches, 1612,
by Thomas Potts

p.3

On the 29th day of March in the year 1612
Abraham Law took Alizon Device to see his
father, John Law the pedlar. He accused the
woman of placing a spell on the old man.
Alizon Device admitted it was true. She fell on
her knees and begged John Law to forgive her.

At the trial Alizon admitted she was guilty
of causing John Law's illness. Alizon's son
James was called as a witness. He said his
mother was a witch and had as her 'familiar' a
brown dog called 'Ball'. Then her nine-year-old
daughter, Jennet, told the judge her mother
was a witch.

I couldn't believe what I was reading. "Alizon
admitted she was a witch?"

"Yes," Ellie groaned. "Just like Gran!"

"But they didn't believe the word of a nine-year-
old girl, did they?" I asked Gary.

"Yes! Remember King James was on the throne. He changed the law. He said that children should be believed in cases of witchcraft!"

"She had no chance," I muttered.

"Neither does Mrs Goonwilde," Pete said. "If she goes out there and admits she's a witch then they'll set fire to her house."

Mrs Goonwilde looked out of the window at the crowds gathering by her railings. "I'll just pop out now and tell them, shall I?"

"No!" we cried together and pulled her back. "You just keep making your soup," I said, "and we'll sort them out."

"Oh, it's not soup!" she said and showed me the recipe book. "It's a spell to help me fly."

# *Flying*

You will need:
  Deadly nightshade
  Wolfsbane
  Henbane
  Hemlock

❖ Crush the flowers together in a bowl until they make a paste.
❖ Smear the paste all over the body.
❖ Sit astride a broomstick.

❖ Recite this spell:
  Horse and hattock,
  Horse and go,
  Horse and pelatis, Ho, ho!

❖ Fly
  (Don't try this
  at home!)

"After all, it is Hallowe'en," Mrs Goonwilde said. "That's what they've all came to see, isn't it? I'd hate to let them down."

"We could have a bit of a problem there," Gary told me.

Mrs Goonwilde, like Alizon Device four hundred years before, was old and ill if she believed her own witchcraft. "No problem, trust me," I said. "Let's all go outside," I said, leading Pete, Gary and Ellie to the door. I slipped the key from the lock, led the others out of the door and locked it behind us. "That'll keep her out of trouble. Now let's go and face that mob out there."

# Chapter 9
# Plans and wigs and water

This was the plan: we dressed Pete as the old woman with a wig, black dress and black shawl over his head so no-one would know. We would offer to duck him in the swimming-tank as a test of his witch powers.

If the crowd were really stupid enough to want that then we would tie Pete's right thumb to his left big toe and take him behind the tank. Then came the clever part (the part I thought of). We'd switch Pete for a dummy dressed the same way. It was ready with bricks from the rubble to weigh it down.

When the dummy was thrown into the water it would sink – the witch would be innocent. We'd drag the dummy out at the back of the tank and put the wet shawl over Pete's head. Then we'd take him quickly back into the house.

Brilliant, you have to agree.

As we led Pete out of the front door the lights flared and the crowd began to cheer as if they were at a football match. A heavy man with a thick bandage around his head stood at the front. I knew from the newspaper photograph this was Doug Down, the injured crane-driver. He grinned a yellow-toothed grin at us and rattled a box of matches. As I stood in front of the water-tank the crowd fell silent. Even the fancy-dress witches came down off the rubble to watch.

"Ladies and gentlemen!" I called. "Mrs Goonwilde here cursed Mr Down and he was hurt."

"Yeah! That's witchcraft, that is!" the crane-driver shouted and the mob cheered him.

"I can explain what happened!" I cried over the howling. "In 1584 a man called Reginald Scot wrote a short book called *The Discoverie of Witchcraft*. It explains everything!"

I pulled a piece of paper from my pocket – a copy of Scot's book that I'd found that afternoon. I read aloud from it...

### THE DISCOVERIE OF WITCHCRAFT

Poor old women go from door to door for a pot of milk. Without it they could hardly live. It happens that sometimes they are refused because the house owner is tired of being pestered by the old witch. So the old woman curses one of the family, then another, until in the end she has cursed the master, his wife, his children and the cattle.

In time some of her neighbours fall sick, or their cattle die, and they imagine it is the revenge of the witch. The witch, on the other hand, sees one in a hundred of her curses come true. She starts to believe that she caused the accident and she admits she was to blame. So she, the family and the law are all tricked!

[6]

The crowd listened in silence. Then Doug Down turned slowly and sneered. "You lot going to believe some dead old bloke? Or are you going to believe me?"

"I believe you!" a man in a donkey-jacket called back.

"So? What we gonna do?" the crane-driver asked.

"Throw the old woman in the tank and burn her house!" his friend shouted back.

The two men began to walk towards Pete, dressed as an old woman. I couldn't uncover his head and show them it was all a trick – and I couldn't let them throw Pete into the water. Pete's couldn't even swim as well as one of the bricks in the dummy!

"Wait! We'll do the ducking trial!" I cried.

"Oh no you won't," Doug Down told me and lunged towards Pete.

I dragged Pete back towards the door, pushed him through and slammed it shut. I turned to face the mob that were pressing forward. Doug Down loomed over me and threw me aside. "If the witch won't be tried then she must be guilty! And we know what you do to witches, don't we?" he roared and rattled the matchbox over his head.

"Burn them!" the mob screamed.

"Burn them!" Doug yelled back. He pulled a newspaper from his pocket and struck a match. If the house caught fire then Pete and Mrs Goonwilde would both die horribly. My plan wasn't meant to work out like this.

"You're wrong! I'll bet you didn't know this!" Gary Grint shouted and snatched the newspaper from Doug Down's hand.

"You what?"

Gary pushed a sheet of paper into the man's dirty hands. "What's this? The Pendle Witches?"

"Yes! Read it!" Gary pleaded.

From The Trial of the Pendle Witches, 1612,
by Thomas Potts
p.4

On the 19th day of August 1612 the judge declared that Alizon Device and her children and friends were guilty of witchcraft. The next day they were taken to Lancaster Moor to the east of the city and there they were all hanged by the neck until they were dead.

"You see!" Gary cried. "No witches were ever burned in England! They burned them in Scotland and they burned them in Germany and lots of other countries – but the English always hanged their witches!"

Nice try, Gary, I thought, but it was too late to stop this crazy crowd now.

"You can't burn the house down!" Gary begged.

Someone passed the crane-driver a can of paraffin. "Who can't?" Doug Down laughed and struck a match.

"You can't!" said a quiet voice from the gate. Everyone swung round and looked at the small, clean-scrubbed girl who stood astride a gleaming golden bicycle.

If Gary couldn't stop the burning then I didn't see how Mabel could…

# Chapter 10
# The flying witch of Nightmare Avenue

Mabel looked into the fierce glare of the lights and the fiercer faces of the excited crowd. "Do excuse me," she said and silenced them with a glare. "But you have come here to see some magic tonight?"

"Yeah!" came the answer.

Mabel nodded and lunged forward. She grabbed Doug Down by the wrist and dragged him forward. "This man says he was cursed by a witch."

"I was!" the man said with a scowl. "She made me crane move and split me head open from ear to ear! I'm lucky to be alive!"

"Then let me show you some real magic," Mabel said and she grabbed an end of the bandage and pulled. The crane-driver spun like a top and came to a staggering, dizzy, cross-eyed stop. His bare head was bald as a billiard ball and it shone in the light. There wasn't a mark on it. "See! I've cured you!"

Doug Down's beady little eyes rolled around like marbles on a playground. "Ah! You must be a witch then!"

Mabel gave a grim smile. "Either that or your head was never hurt in the first place."

"You what?"

"You lied!"

"Why would I do that?"

"Same as all the other people in history lied about witches... for what you could get out of it!" I shouted. Now I could see Mabel's cunning plan, you understand. It wasn't as good as my plan – it just happened to be working a little better.

The crane-driver clenched his huge fists and looked at me. "Oh, yeah, Miss Smarty-knickers. And why would I want to do that?"

"To drive Mrs Goonwilde out of her house so the road could be built!" Gary Grint said, catching on to the wicked-witch plot.

"I'm just a crane-driver!" Doug Down cried to the mob of people who were starting to shuffle their feet and look a lot less excited now.

"But somebody paid you to fake the accident, you extremely hairless man," Mabel said. "Pity the records at Duckpool hospital fail to show you went there for treatment."

"So what?"

"So… you could probably go to prison for causing a public disturbance – stirring up all these people to attack an old lady in her home," Mabel said calmly. "You could probably go to prison for a couple of years."

"Or fifty!" I put in.

"It's not fair!" Doug Down wailed.

"No – it's the fault of the person who paid you," Gary Grint said. "Tell us the name!"

The man clasped his hands to his bald head and looked up towards the television cameras. "I'm innocent! Innocent, I tell you! I'm not to blame – I was put up to this by…"

"There's no need for all this!" came a sharp voice from the back of the crowd. A small man with a gold chain around his neck stepped forward.

"Daddy!" Mabel exclaimed.

"Yes, my little rosebud," the mayor said, wrapping an arm around his daughter's shoulder. "You have done well with your Time Detectives. But it is my pleasure to tell you that Mrs Goonwilde's house is safe! Duckpool Council decided tonight that the two lanes of the new road can go around either side of the house. Together we have saved a harmless old lady!"

Two minutes before, the crowd had been cheering the idea of burning down the house on Nightmare Avenue. Now they cheered because the house was saved. Crowds can be like that, Miss Toon says.

"Who paid Doug Down?" I demanded.

Mayor Tweed spread his hands and smiled. "Who knows?"

The crane-driver had slipped away quickly into the darkness behind the television lights and into the safe black cloak of night.

Steadily the crowd began to melt into the darkness of Nightmare Avenue. The little witches and monsters found their parents and headed home, tired and strangely quiet. Then a voice high above them cried, "I can fly!"

The television lights swung upwards to the window at the top of Mrs Goonwilde's house. Ellie's gran had thrown open the window and pushed her twig broom out. She cried, "Horse and hattock, Horse and go, Horse and pelatis, Ho, ho!"

Then she jumped.

The witch of Nightmare Avenue flew. She seemed to hang in the air for half a second, then she flew – straight down into the garden.

# Chapter 11

# Nurses for nightmares

"Thank goodness the water-tank broke her fall," Miss Toon said next day when she met the Time Detectives.

"She's a bit shaken," Ellie said. "They'll keep her in hospital for a week."

Miss Toon took the large girl's hands in her own. "You've done well to look after her for so long, Ellie. But now you need help – you can't go on missing school and she needs an expert to look after her. When she comes out of hospital she can go home to Lord Mayor Avenue – but she'll have to have a nurse to visit every day."

Ellie nodded. "She's not well, I know. She started to really believe she had magic powers. It was scary."

Miss Toon explained, "She has something called senile dementia, Ellie. It happens to some old people. When it does we have to take special care of them."

"Is that what happened to witches in the days of King James?" I asked.

The teacher nodded.
"It would explain why old people were often accused of being witches – they began acting strangely and even began to believe in the old superstitions."

"Then greedy people came along and tried to take advantage of them. Drive them out of their homes and take them over," I said.

"Not witchcraft, then?" Pete Plank said slowly. "Just greed."

"And Mrs Goonwilde showed that's something that never changes," I said. "I wonder who paid Doug Down to start that story? Mayor Tweed interrupted before we could find out!"

"Daddy's a millionaire," Mabel said quickly. She was looking down at the floor and seemed to be a little embarrassed. "And he owns part of the road-building company. He says he's going to pay for the nurse and anything else that Mrs Goonwilde needs!"

I didn't need to be a Time Detective to work out why. Gary understood and he looked at me. I shook my head. Pete was struggling to think it out.

"So, Mrs Goonwilde's story will have a happier ending than some of the witchcraft victims of the past," Miss Toon said. "Now you've done a fascinating project and I want you to work out a way of presenting it in next week's school assembly."

"Uhh?" Pete grunted. "Where we say prayers and things? I don't know any prayers."

"Here's one," Gary said. " I found it in one of the research books. It seems that not everyone in King James's day was as stupid as the king. They didn't all believe in witchcraft. They were horrified by what they saw – especially the way helpless old women were treated – so they wrote this prayer."

And that's how the Time Detectives brought the case of the Witch of Nightmare Avenue to a close. With that prayer written four hundred years ago...

For all those who died - stripped naked, shaved, shorn.

For those who screamed in vain to God, only to have their tongues ripped out by the root.

For those who were pricked, racked, broken on the wheel for the sins of the witch-hunters.

For those whose beauty stirred their torturers to fury.

For those whose ugliness did the same.

For those who were neither ugly nor beautiful, but only women who would not confess.

For those quick fingers broken in the vice.

For those soft arms pulled from their sockets.

For all those witch-women, my sisters, who breathed freer as the flames took them, knowing as they shed their female bodies, that death would shed them of the sin for which they died - the sin of being born a woman.

# Time trail

1567    James Stuart becomes King James VI of Scotland
        when he's still a baby. Powerful lords struggle to
        control him and control the country. The wizard
        Earl of Bothwell threatens James with witchcraft.

1584    Sensible Reginald Scot writes a short book called
        *The Discoverie of Witchcraft* to show that witches
        don't exist. James, who thinks he knows better,
        writes *Demonologie* to prove that they do.

1590    When James sails back from Denmark with his
        new queen he is caught in a terrible storm. He
        believes witches, led by Agnes Sampson, are to
        blame and under torture the witches confess.

1603    James becomes King James I of England and
        changes English laws so witches can be caught
        and executed. He also says that child witnesses
        should be believed in witchcraft trials.

1605    James has other enemies apart from witches. The Catholics hate him and Guy Fawkes is caught in a plot to blow him up.

1606    William Shakespeare wants to please the new King James (what a creep) so he writes a play about witchcraft. It is called *Macbeth* and shows how James's family overcame the power of witches 500 years before.

1612    One of the gunpowder plotters has Catholic relatives in Lancashire. James doesn't trust people from that county. How can Lancashire people show their loyalty to the king? Bring some witches to trial! Alizon Device and her family are arrested. Nine-year-old Jennet gives evidence against her mother – but remember, James said that is all right – and ten women and one man are hanged.

1615    James says he's changing his mind about witches now. Maybe they don't exist after all. But they are still being caught and executed.

1625    James dies but his Stuart childen still rule over witch trials.

1644    A man called Matthew Hopkin claims he can find witches. English towns pay him a lot of money to find their witches and he finds 400 before he is finally shown to be a liar and a cheat.

1684    The last witch is hanged in England but it is not until…

1727    …the last witch is burned in Scotland and…

1775    …the last witch is burned in Germany.